The Gift

The Gift

Aletha Hinthorn

90 Minute Books
Atlanta, Georgia

Library of Congress Cataloging in Publication Data:
ISNB
Printed in the United States of America

10 9 8 7 6 5 4 3 2

Thank you, Jesus, for giving us the gift of blessing others through prayer.

Table of Contents

God, Show Me You Care

"The Lord is my rock, my fortress and my deliverer; my God is my rock, in whom I take refuge. He is my shield and the horn of my salvation, my stronghold" *(Psalm 18:2).*

When the songwriter wrote, "Does Jesus care?" he was asking the question we most long to hear answered. He speaks in amazing ways to those who listen.

Nancy has a 25-year-old daughter who had three children out of wedlock with two different men who were abusive and addicted to drugs. She has since moved away from the most recent man and is living on her own rearing these children. One day Nancy's heart was especially heavy for her daughter and three grandchildren. While driving home from the school where she had taken her grandchildren, she cried out to the Lord to protect them.

Just then a mother duck walked into traffic, leading her three little ducklings across the road. Nancy stopped to let them pass, and then an oncoming car swerved to miss hitting them. The next car was a policeman who pulled his car into both lanes of traffic and turned on his lights waiting for the ducks to cross in safety. Once they got across the road everyone returned to business as usual.

As Nancy was driving away, she glimpsed the ducks in her rearview mirror, and the Lord seemed to say, "Nancy, look how I protected that mother duck and her three ducklings. Look at the people I put in place to assure their safety, and look how I positioned you to have a front row seat to witness it all. Don't you think I could do far more for your daughter and her three children? Trust me in this!" Nancy was deeply touched by God's eyewitness lesson. Jesus cared!

Our psychiatrist friend shared that for a while he went through a period of deep depression. One day he prayed, "God, You are all I've got. Show me You love me."

Soon after his prayer, his wife and son went out of town. He went to a bookstore to get a book on world-class soccer. As he walked through the store, he noticed a lot of pornography.

The thought came to him. This is the best chance I'll have. It's a weekday and no one else is in here. He began glancing through Playboy and Penthouse and picked up a couple to buy. When he did, he heard, "You can't do this." Surprised, he put them down. Then he reconsidered. "I really wanted those magazines," he admitted. He again picked them up and again heard clearly and so forcibly it was almost frightening, "You cannot do this."

Reluctantly he put them down, paid for his book, and left the bookstore.

He had walked only a few feet outside when someone called to him. It was a patient he had been treating for pornography. Our friend greeted him and the patient asked what he had bought. With unspeakable relief he showed him the book on world-class soccer! At that moment, he knew God, in His love, had delivered him from a potential embarrassing and harmful situation!

Marcy shared that she and her extended family had met in the mountains for a family reunion. One morning she awakened, praying for all the children in the family—her own plus her nieces and nephews. Later she wondered if her prayers had made any difference. Was God really listening?

Later that day there was an accident at the park as the children rode up a gondola and then rode down on bicycles. Only two were injured. Another boy got lost but had taken someone's cell phone with him so he was able to call his mother.

The next day, as the adults reflected on how much worse the day could have been, someone said, "God was all over that mountain protecting our children." Then Marcy knew. Yes, God had heard her prayers.

One of my favorite songs to sing in private worship is "There's a Wideness in God's Mercy." Recently I found another version that includes a verse I had not seen before:

"There's no place where earth's sorrows
Are felt more than they are in heaven;
There's no place where earth's failings
Have such kindly judgment given."

Frederick Faber ends this song with these words:
"If our love were but more simple
We should take Him at His word;
And our lives would be all sunshine

13

In the goodness of the Lord."
Nothing brings sunshine to our lives more than a fresh awareness that Jesus cares.

> *Dear Jesus,*
>
> *I praise You because You are more aware of my needs than I am. Your care for me is perfect even when I am unaware of Your presence. Thank You for feeling my sorrows and giving me victory over temptation. I find great joy when I trust in Your unfailing kindness. Thank You for always caring for me. In Jesus' name, Amen.*

Discussion Questions

1. Have you ever doubted God's care for you? Think about ways God has demonstrated His care for you in the past. Share your experience with others.

2. Have you ever prayed, "God, show me You love me"? How can this kind of prayer take you beyond simply having personal devotions to knowing God?

3. Consider Psalm 18:2. How does this Scripture widen your vision of who God is?

Our Real Work

"Speak, LORD, for your servant is listening" (I Samuel 3:9).

Some years ago, I saw an ad for *The Wall Street Journal* that said, "If you don't read *The Wall Street Journal,* you are saving a little time—when you could be investing it."

Nothing is a better investment of time than prayer. When the well-known Evangelism Explosion program began expanding into new churches, the director made an important discovery. Even though the program was working well, he asked each church to enlist two church members to pray for each Evangelism Explosion worker, especially on Tuesday nights when the program was in operation. The evangelist reported back to his two intercessors weekly. They discovered that when intercessors prayed, the number of professions of faith doubled!"

"Jesus often withdrew to lonely places and prayed," states Luke 5:16. The next verse comments,

"As he was teaching...the power of the Lord was present." Perhaps there's a connection between these two verses. He often withdrew to lonely places and prayed even when He could have been teaching. Then when He taught, His power was evident.

Our real work is prayer. The reason is simple. Only after we've brought our need to God, discerned how to ask specifically, and persevered until He helped us believe, can we rest from our own works and enter into His. Only then do we have power to discern and obey His will. Without investing time in prayer, we proceed in our own strength and do things in a way that seems right to us. How often God's ways are so far beyond ours that we would never dream of them in a hundred years.

Last weekend I heard a story about my Grandmother Wehrman that occurred over 50 years ago. A cousin, Lydia Knipmeyer, who recently went to be with the Lord, told in her final testimony in church how she had been converted as a young girl.

One night about 2 o'clock in the morning, my grandmother walked the six miles from our farm to Lydia's parents' farm in the cold Missouri winter and announced, "I have come to pray for Lydia to be saved." Lydia's father, my grandmother's brother, awakened the entire household and they all gathered around Lydia and prayed. Lydia did not get saved that night, but the next day, she went to the hayloft where she intended to pray quietly so no one would hear her. She became so earnest that her intentions were forgotten and she prayed so loudly everyone heard her. She left the loft that day knowing her sins were forgiven.

Grandmother's nighttime visit seemed to have brought a spirit of revival. Within weeks more of my cousins came to the Lord. One of those was August

Luelf, who is also now in heaven, but was loved and known by thousands as "the stuttering preacher." Another was Wesley Duewel. His books have been printed in 57 languages and over two million copies have been sold.

Not only will His power be present when we make prayer our work but also we hear His voice. "Be still and know that I am God" (Psalm 46:10). A deep inner knowing flows out of being still. After Jesus withdrew into lonely places and prayed, He had power to discern the Pharisees' thoughts and to say to the paralytic, "Get up and walk." Grandmother Wehrman prayed until she knew she was to walk through the night to pray for Lydia.

The Quakers spoke of an "inner stillness." As we learn to be still and know God, the Holy Spirit gives an increased clearness to our thinking. His speaking, always gentle and deeply interior, provides us with grace, wisdom, and power to do His work.

Time in His presence also renews our strength. Recently I went to bed one Saturday night feeling overwhelmed because of four uncompleted projects. When I awakened early on Sunday morning, I opened my Bible to Jeremiah 30 and read verse 22. "So you will be my people, and I will be your God." I began considering what it means for God to be my God. He is in charge of all I do. He provides the resources, time, ideas, and even the energy. In fact, He says we will lack nothing. As I stayed there in His presence and thought on His promise to be my God, my rest returned.

The stress, burnout, and pressures of life disappear when we seek God until we find Him. The resulting tranquility of spirit is the true resort. We don't need a Florida vacation to find this inner rest, just an investment of time alone with the Lord.

If you don't take time to be still in His presence, you are saving a little time—when you could be investing it.

Dear Lord God,

Thank you for the marvelous dividends that come when I spend time in Your presence. Help me to remember that my real work for You is not in 'doing,' but in 'being' in Your presence. Only then am I fully satisfied. Today, I wait upon You to empower me to do Your plans and to give me Your wisdom. In Jesus' name, Amen.

Discussion Questions

1. What keeps you from doing your "real work?" What lifestyle adjustments might waiting upon God require?

2. How might Jesus' example of withdrawing to a "lonely place to pray" motivate and encourage you to actually make those changes?

3. Give a personal illustration of how God has empowered you to do His work by means of taking time in His presence.

Desperate Praying

"Blessed are those who hunger and thirst for righteousness, for they will be filled" (Matthew 5:6).

A pastor recently recalled being in a prayer meeting in a small room in South America with about 60 others who were earnestly calling out to God. As he listened to them pray for two hours, he thought, they have something I don't. As he pondered that prayer meeting the next few days, the word "desperation" kept coming to him. These people, desperate for God to answer their prayers, prayed with fervency that his prayers often lacked.

Desperate praying will be shown in many ways. Although it may mean praying with others for two hours, it sometimes means praying the same request consistently over weeks, months, or even years. For six years a missionary to China has been asking, seeking, and knocking for an open door to the closed country of North Korea. He recently wrote of his passion for this country. "Deep feeling brings fervency to prayer like dry wood supplies flames to fire. The understanding that never-dying souls in North Korea are perishing daily because of the obstructive leadership there should wring out of our hearts urgent and heated prayers of intercession to God for a quick resolution to this awful situation. Thus I am praying, and unashamedly ask for you to join us in this spiritual battle. Progress is being made but the balance has not yet tipped. Let's pray until God's spiritual forces victoriously make their way onto the streets of Pyongyang!"

Desperate praying can also mean determining to pray until we know God has heard, or as it is sometimes called, "praying through." One evening years ago when our daughter Arla was about two years old, she was playing on the patio behind our house. Suddenly I heard her cry, and she came in terrified.

"Goggle-man, Mommy, goggle-man," she sobbed. I didn't know what goggle-man meant, but I understood that some man had frightened her. (Years later she remembered him as a man on a motorcycle.)

When my husband came home, he asked, "Is everything all right? Coming home tonight I had the feeling that you were in danger."

I told him about the goggle-man and then we recalled discovering that the chain on our back gate had been cut that week. Did someone plan to harm our daughter?

We put the children to bed and then knelt to pray. We had to have God's protection even if it meant praying all night. Praying all night was not necessary, however, for praying earnestly we soon received an assurance that all would be well. Perhaps the rest God brought to my over-anxious mind was as much a miracle as the safety of our daughter He also provided. The debilitating fears that can follow such incidents were simply not there for either my daughter or me.

Although the term "praying through" is not in the Bible, the concept is found in the definition of faith. "Now faith is being sure of what we hope for and certain of what we do not see" (Hebrews 11:1). It is seeing with our spiritual eyes the evidence not yet visible with our physical eyes. Faith includes the evidence or the inner knowledge that our prayer is answered.

Desperate praying sometimes includes fasting food or fasting sleep. Jesus promised that those who engage in secret fasting would be openly rewarded (Matthew 6:18). Results will come, but they are not always immediate or predictable. At times, results are gradual and tend to diversify as we give ourselves more and more to fasting. God may not respond to our fasts in the way we anticipate, but He will keep His promise to openly reward us.

God's ears are open to desperate praying. "'Even now,' declares the Lord, 'return to me with all your heart, with fasting and weeping and mourning.'… Who knows? He may turn and have pity and leave behind a blessing" (Joel 2:12, 14).

Isaiah wrote, "Oh that you would burst from the heavens and come down!" Let's join in desperately praying that God will do awesome things beyond our highest expectations.

Dear Heavenly Father,

Fill me with such a hunger and thirst for the things that are on Your heart that I will pray earnestly and persistently until I receive Your answers. I long to see miracles in my

*life, in my family, and throughout this
land. In Jesus' name, Amen.*

Discussion Questions

1. How does desperate praying go beyond having personal devotions?

2. Why do you think "praying through" is difficult for many believers?

3. What "deep feeling" do you experience that God may use to give birth to desperate praying?

Faith Does the Impossible

"The prayer of a righteous man is powerful and effective" (James 5:16).

Becky Schenck, a missionary in Papua New Guinea, described an incredible incident. One of the nationals was stabbed to death in a tavern one Saturday night. The next morning her husband, Jerry, and another missionary went to the scene with some national Christians hoping to help.

The tribal custom in Papua New Guinea demands that if a member of the tribe dies, someone from the murderer's tribe must die as a payback. Older men had been training younger men to fight for such an occasion. Now, with war-painted faces and carrying their bows and arrows, and spears and axes, they were approaching the tribe of the murderer.

The angry mob came to the government officer who was trying to block the road with his car to prevent the confrontation. They threw him in the ditch and marched on.

With much fear and trembling, Jerry and the other Christian nationals formed a "human road-block" while the other missionary stood on the hood of the car praying. The angry tribal members came within inches of them.

Suddenly they stopped, turned around, and went back!

The next day the missionaries learned why. The warring tribal members said they had looked at the man on the car praying and their bodies felt weak, as if they had been doing a hard day's work. They had no energy to go farther.

We rarely get to glimpse the amazing effect of our prayers. God's response to our prayers renders the enemy powerless to discourage, to attack, to tempt, but we cannot see God at work. We simply trust that He is. One of the greatest wonders in Heaven for us may be the complete dependability of God to answer our prayers.

After years on the mission field, Jonathan Goforth visited his prayer partner in London, telling her of the great revival movements he had experienced in China. She invited him to look at her prayer diary. With great joy, they discovered that the times of her special intercession for him corresponded exactly to the times of his greatest revivals.

I've been amazed at times when I've talked with someone for whom I've been praying and learned that God was working precisely as I had been asking. Adoniram Judson said, "I never prayed sincerely and earnestly for anything, but that it came at some time—no matter how distant a day, somehow, in some shape, probably the last I would have devised, it came." All who pray with faith find that God is faithful. Sometimes we fail, but God never fails.

This week I was praying for someone in a cult, and the Holy Spirit reminded me that Jesus came in when "the doors were being shut." When we pray, God makes the enemy powerless. He still goes in where He's been locked out.

Dear Almighty God,

Increase my faith to ask you to do the seemingly impossible. I trust that You, O God, will thwart each plan that opposes Your will and establish only those that will give You glory. In Jesus' name, Amen.

Discussion Questions

1. God's Word offers a multitude of promises that can steady our faith and destroy our fears. Read and consider the following: Psalm 33:8-22; Psalm 34:15-19; 2 Chronicles 20:5-12; Joshua 1:1-9; Isaiah 65:24; Lamentations 3:22-26. How do these truths speak to your troubles today?

2. Share a time when you prayed in faith for God to move in a difficult situation. What were the effects and how did it affect your prayer life?

3. What is the condition that makes our prayers "powerful and effective" according to James 5:16?

Learning to Listen

"I am the good shepherd, I know my sheep and my sheep know me...They too will listen to my voice" (John 10:14,16b).

For decades Evelyn Christensen has gone around the world encouraging women to pray. During this time, her own prayer life has deepened. She was asked, "How much time do you spend each day in prayer?"

Her reply was, "Two hours is threadbare. My goal is to pray 24 hours. By that I don't mean saying words, but keeping communication open."

"He who unites himself with the Lord is one with him in spirit," Paul wrote to the Corinthians. If we are one in our spirits with the Lord, why should it ever be difficult to keep the communication open? Could it be that "walking in the Spirit" is a learned pattern? The sheep learn to identify the shepherd's voice by being with the shepherd. We must be alone with Him until our souls are at rest in His presence and we hear Him speak. Then the Holy Spirit will move through us almost unnoticed except that He's causing us to love by softening our attitudes and giving us His desires.

In her book *Open Heart, Open Home*, Karen Mains writes, "I have come to learn how important it is to sit in silence before my Maker. The time for words and pleas and explanations is over. The Word has been studied and now the pages are shut. Now to listen. Now to keep one's mind fixed on Him. Now to be silent. Often when I leave these times of contemplation I am filled with His Presence." As we come again and again for this renewing of God's presence, our sensitivity to the Holy Spirit increases. Our ability to hear God in our prayer closets determines our ability to hear Him throughout our day.

"Surely the Lord was in this place and I did not know it," we could cry with Jacob. The Holy Spirit is with us moment by moment, but we do not have our "senses exercised to discern" His presence. Our need is to develop a continual dependency upon Him and to constantly be aware of His guidance, His impulses, His hesitancies.

I've been amazed to find that He's always willing to lead when I lift my thoughts to Him. It's when I rush on ahead, ignoring God within me, that I make wrong decisions and say words that "fall to the ground."

When we are made aware of His Presence and His counsel and wait in faith for His plans to unfold, He actually leads and controls. But when we treat Him in our thought life with neglect, as though He's not present, He is grieved and quenched.

Moses discovered the secret of being Spirit-led. He constantly saw Him who is invisible (Hebrews

11:27). This continual beholding Him, who is invisible, will be the secret of our lives in learning to discern God's personal leadings.

Dear Lord,

I love sitting in Your presence and hearing You speak through Your Word. In Your presence I learn to identify Your voice. Then what a joy to live in You and have Your counsel even in the midst of my busy day. In Jesus' name, Amen.

Discussion Questions

1. Prayer is more than saying words. It's keeping communication open with God, moment by moment, throughout the day. Brother Lawrence calls it "practicing His presence." How is this kind of prayer life to be nurtured?

2. "He who unites himself with the Lord is one with him in spirit." What obstacles stand in your way to this kind of uniting? Stop and confess them, asking for God's mercy and grace.

3. When you come to God in your prayer closet, sitting silent, listening for His voice, what do you hear Him say to you?

Pray With Thanksgiving

"Give thanks in all circumstances, for this is God's will for you in Christ Jesus" (1 Thessalonians 5:18).

"There are few times I don't feel like praising the Lord," my mother said.

I should not have been surprised. Mother hardly ever said aloud, "Praise the Lord." Yet, because of her consistently joyful spirit, I could easily believe she carried a thankful spirit.

What was her secret? Had she merely disciplined herself to feel thankful? Or was her thankful spirit a natural result of some aspect of her Christian life? I thought about these questions as I recently read Paul's letter to the Colossians and noticed his repeated command to always be thankful. How did mother do that?

Even though Paul wrote from a prison cell, he said he always gave thanks when he prayed for the Colossians. He prayed they, too, would joyfully give thanks and asked them to overflow with thankfulness. He asked them to sing to God with thankful hearts and to give thanks in everything they said or did. Finally, he asked them to devote themselves to prayer with a thankful heart (Colossians 1:3, 11-12; 2:7; 3:15-17; 4:2). That's a tall order. Evidently Paul, too, believed there are times we don't feel like praising the Lord.

As I read these verses, a prayer formed in my heart: "How can I be one who is always thankful and who always prays with thankfulness?"

The Spirit reminded me of Paul's words in Colossians 3:1-2: "Set your hearts on things above, where Christ is seated at the right hand of God. Set your minds on things above, not on earthly things."

Paul had done that. His heart and mind were set on Christ, and he described Christ as having all the honor of one seated at the right hand of God: "By him all things were created; things in heaven and on earth, visible and invisible, whether thrones or powers or rulers or authorities; all things were created by him and for him. He is before all things, and in him all things hold together" (1:16, 18).

Mother, too, loved to think about her great God. Her favorite song was "How Great Thou Art." During her last months, the book *High Conceptions of God* was often beside her Bible. She had set her heart and her mind on things above. The result was a spirit of worship and praise.

When we don't feel like praising the Lord, giving thanks might be the last thing we want to do. It is then time to respond to Paul's words: "Set your mind and keep them set on what is above" (Colossians 3:2 Amplified) We can and must choose where we will place our thoughts.

Here are three practical suggestions.

The psalmist tells us to "Enter his gates with thanksgiving" (Psalm 100:4). We can do what one young man told me he did during a difficult time. Throughout his day he kept a yellow note pad close by and recorded anything he thought of for which he could praise the Lord. The next morning during his devotions, he would set his timer for five minutes and begin thanking God for the things he had written down the day before. He said, "Within three minutes, I was 'in the gate' and by the end of the five minutes, His presence would wash over me."

Another help is to make sure that we are thinking of God. Paul didn't just say, "I'm thankful for you" but "I thank my God" (Philippians 1:3), not doubting God's goodness and power. It is easy to give thanks for something and hardly think of Him at all.

Thinking of "my God" as Paul did brings an attitude of worship. When we do this, our gloom disappears and our spirit rises as we think on God and what He has done and what His Word promises. If I allow my mind to continually dwell on problems I am praying about, it can be quite a stretch from there to always give thanks. But it seems to be a small step from thanking Him with a truly grateful heart for His good and perfect plans for the future to trusting Him to indeed fulfill those plans. What joy such confidence provides! It's the thankful-to-God spirit that is a joyful spirit. No wonder the theme of Philippians (another epistle written in prison) is joy! Paul was always thankful!

A third suggestion is to remember Paul's admonition to give "thanks through [Christ] to God the Father." The Spirit of Christ within us is a spirit of thanksgiving. To always be giving thanks is simply to respond to His Spirit living within us!

Dear Lord,

Today I choose to dwell on what is right, good, lovely, and of good report. Thank You that You help me to take every thought captive and make it obedient to Christ, pleasing to You. With Your help, I can replace negative and critical thoughts with thoughts of Your goodness and power. In Jesus' name, Amen.

Discussion Questions

1. Have I disciplined myself to be thankful? What is my usual response to testings and trials?

2. When I don't feel like giving thanks, what three things can I do to help refocus my thoughts on "what is above?"

3. Make a "thankful list" beginning right now. What will I tell God I am thankful for today?

Prayer Gives So Much

"Devote yourselves to prayer, being watchful and thankful" (Colossians 4:2).

In November 1995, my husband Daniel and I went to Los Angeles to attend "Fasting and Prayer '95" organized by Dr. Bill Bright of Campus Crusade for Christ. More than 3,500 people gathered for this historic event of nearly 20 hours of prayer and three days of fasting.

On Thursday night we entered the huge Los Angeles Convention Center where the chairs were arranged in circles of ten. For three hours that evening, twelve hours the next day, and three hours on Saturday, we sang, worshipped, and listened to speakers, but mainly we prayed in our small groups of ten. Each of the speakers talked for five minutes, and then we spent 15 minutes praying about the subject he or she had addressed.

The first evening Dr. Ruibal of Cali, Colombia, South America, reported that 22,000 Christians fasted and prayed all night for their city of Cali. Within 48 hours, police arrested a primary drug lord from the Cali Cartel. Many others were soon arrested, causing the demise of the entire Cali drug ring.

Although many of the speakers were well-known Christian leaders, often instead of being introduced, their names would simply appear on a large screen. "We have left our résumés at the door," the emcee announced. On the last morning, a lady in our small group said, "Instead of going away impressed that I was able to hear a well-known speaker, all I think about is God."

For me, the highlight was meeting Nancy, a petite Vietnamese woman in our circle. God has called her to be an intercessor. I loved it when she prayed! It seemed that Nancy always prayed what the Holy Spirit wanted us to request for the need that had just been addressed.

Nancy has given permission to share what she sent me after we returned home.

"In January 1991, God called me to enter a ministry of intercession. I had to step down from both my part-time job and teaching a ladies' Bible study group at a local church. I did not fully understand. But His voice was clear enough for me to obey. There was no need to discuss the decision with flesh and blood.

"Then God called me to deeper repentance in order for me to move closer to His heart. As His heart beat heavily upon mine, I began to weep for America. At times He wailed and groaned through me for this nation and for the world as well.

"Besides my daily hours of intercessory prayer, He led me to promote prayer among the women in the local church and friends in other parts of the country who have expressed a similar concern. God allowed me to see lives changed much faster than I had before through a Bible study. People who have never known how to pray or had little interest in prayer have become leaders in the school of prayer. My name has never been printed on a bulletin or even mentioned in public for this ministry, but God has let me witness some of His mighty works in the lives of His people for whom I prayed."

"Since that day [in Los Angeles] my heart has burned more intensively for revival in America. The Lord has shown me that our labor will be in vain if we ourselves are not being revived and renewed. I strongly feel that God has revealed to me that He wants to use me as an instrument for the coming revival for which He has been preparing me for the past five years. He wants me to promote fasting and prayer where I am right now. He will surely lead me as He has in the past five years. 'Lead on, O King Eternal...'"

Nancy's statement that through prayer "God allowed me to see lives changed much faster than through a Bible study" challenged me. For many months I had wondered why the Lord hadn't allowed me to reestablish our neighborhood Bible study. The Lord reminded me that others I know are having Bible studies. If people are changed faster through prayer than through teaching, why not pray for these people rather than teach other classes? Bible teaching is necessary, but God waters those seeds sown by the tears of Bible teachers' intercessory prayers.

Andrew Murray said, "Time spent in prayer will yield more than that given to work." What could be a better use of my time?

Dear Gracious God,

I sit in Your presence asking for personal revival and renewal. I long to be Your instrument of grace, praying prayers that will do exceedingly, abundantly beyond what I can think or imagine. In Jesus' name, Amen.

Discussion Questions

1. According to Nancy, we can pray in vain or pray productive prayers. What will make the difference?

2. Have you ever tried to change something or someone by good efforts and well-meaning intentions? Why is prayer a better way?

3. Give personal examples of good fruit your prayers have yielded.

Secret Choices

"The Lord confides in those who fear Him; he makes his covenant known to them" (Psalm 25:14).

Isobel Kuhn attended Moody Bible Institute for training to become a missionary among the Lisu people in China. The school schedule was busy, especially for those working their way through as Isobel did.

One day the president of a student group came to her with great concern: "It is so easy, with required hours of Bible reading, to let one's own devotional time slip. And it inevitably leads to staleness of soul. Will you pray, Isobel, and ask the Lord for a solution, and give us a talk on it at the next meeting?"

Isobel accepted the burden because she had felt that danger herself. In certain classes students were required to read a book of the Bible. Why read it again for quiet time? But reading the Scriptures for a technical grasp and reading it in the Lord's presence, asking Him to speak, were two different things. As Isobel prayed about the talk, she felt a need to encourage students to form a habit of putting the Lord first each day. She used 2 Chronicles 29:11 for her text: "My sons, do not be negligent now, for the Lord has chosen you to stand before him and serve him, to minister before him and to burn incense" (KJV).

She challenged her classmates to make a covenant with the Lord to spend one hour a day (for about a year) in the Lord's presence, in prayer and reading the Word. The purpose was to form the habit of putting God in the center of their day and fitting the work of life around Him rather than letting the day's business occupy the central place. Isobel put the text and covenant on a sheet of paper and asked how many would sign it.

She suggested the signers meet together once a month to confess any failures and then worship the Lord together. It was a very small meeting and only nine signed that covenant, but news of it spread and others later joined.

To keep her hour-a-day required planning, Isobel would go to the one place she could be undisturbed—the cleaning closet, at 5:30 each morning. She would turn the scrubbing pail upside down, sit on it, and with mops and dust rags hanging around her head, spend a precious half-hour with the Master. After 30 minutes, she went to the dining hall to set tables. The other half-hour had to be found at the end of her day.

At the close of the year, Isobel was asked to lead the devotional at the students' Junior-Senior party and to play the role of a Dutch grandma in a skit. Her previous week had been so full of work and study that she didn't have time to prepare the devotional. On the day of the banquet, her work had delayed her and by suppertime she was hungry, exhausted, and didn't have any devotional prepared. Before she sat down to dinner she realized she had half an hour due on her quiet time. After the party she knew she and the other juniors had to clean up, and she would not get to her room till midnight. The day would be gone.

So she evaluated her choices for the supper hour: should she eat supper, skip supper and prepare a devotional, or give that half-hour to God?

The supper bell rang, and her roommate left for the dining room. Isobel stood for a moment undecided. Then, throwing herself on her knees by her bedside, she sobbed out in a whisper, "Oh, Lord, I choose You!"

Too weary to form words, she just rested in God. Suddenly the sense of His presence filled the room. The weariness left her and she felt relaxed, refreshed, bathed in His love. Isobel said, "As I half-knelt, saying nothing, but just loving Him, drinking in His tenderness, He spoke to me. Quietly, but point by point, He outlined for me the devotional message I needed to close that evening's program."

In the exhilaration of that moment, Isobel ran down to the banquet, slipped into her costume, and went through the program. At the end, she gave very simply the devotional message God had given her during her supper hour. Such a quiet hush came over that festive scene that she knew He had spoken, and she was content.

More than twenty years later, Isobel was home from China, visiting with friends at Moody. It was the day of the Junior-Senior party and a group of her former classmates were reminiscing. "One Junior-

Senior party always stands out in my memory," one said. "I forget who led it but it was a Dutch scene and the devotional blessed my soul. I've never forgotten it." She had indicated the date, so Isobel knew. She was thrilled.

"Of course, I did not spoil it by telling her who led that devotional," Isobel said. "In God's perfect workings the instrument is forgotten. It is the blessing of Himself that is remembered."

Dear Heavenly Father,

I love you! And I choose You! I lay aside everything and every voice that calls for my attention so that I may spend some time alone with You. I realize that only You can fill my soul with peace and rest. There is no sweeter place than in Your Presence. In Jesus' name, Amen.

Discussion Questions

1. If you were given one free hour each day to do of your own choosing, what would you do?

2. Are you spending time diligently reading your Bible and yet still experiencing that "staleness of soul?" How does Isobel's example encourage you?

3. Give an example from your own experience in which giving yourself to prayer resulted in great benefit.

See God's Goodness

← 7-1-18

"And we know that in all things God works for the good of those who love him, who have been called according to his purpose" (Romans 8:28).

Today's email brought a story told by Helen Roseveare, a missionary doctor to Africa. Despite her best efforts, a mother she attended in the labor ward died leaving a tiny baby and a two-year-old daughter. To keep the premature baby warm someone went to fill a hot water bottle. Unfortunately, the bottle broke and they had no other bottles.

The following noon when Dr. Roseveare prayed with the orphanage children she told them about the tiny baby, mentioning the hot water bottle and also the sister, crying because her mother had died.

Ten-year-old Ruth prayed, "Please, God, send us a water bottle. It'll be no good tomorrow, God, as the baby will be dead, so please send it this afternoon."

While Dr. Roseveare gasped inwardly at the audacity of the prayer, Ruth added, "And would You

41

please send a dolly for the little girl so she'll know You really love her?"

How could Dr. Roseveare honestly say, "Amen"? She had been in Africa for almost four years and had never received a parcel from home. And she certainly had nowhere to go to buy these supplies.

But at mid afternoon, a car arrived at her front door and someone left a parcel. She sent for the children, and excitement mounted as she lifted out brightly colored, knitted jerseys, bandages, and a box of raisins.

Then she felt the...could it be? She pulled out a brand-new hot water bottle! Ruth rushed forward, crying, "If God has sent the bottle, He must have sent the dolly, too!"

Rummaging to the bottom of the box, she pulled out a small, beautifully dressed dolly.

That parcel, packed by Dr. Roseveare's former Sunday school class, had been on the way for five months.

Isaiah wrote, "Before they call, I will answer" (65:24). He does this more frequently than we realize. Are you more prone to remember the unanswered prayers you've prayed repeatedly than those God has already answered? Joseph remained in prison for years and he must have prayed many times for deliverance. While in prison "the Lord was with him; he showed him kindness" (Genesis 39:20, 21). God showed him kindness, but not deliverance!

Because God is good, He intends everything He allows to ultimately bring us His kindness. Joseph had been abused by his brothers, separated from his devoted father, falsely accused of immorality, and finally abandoned in prison. Then we hear him say, "But God intended it for good" (Genesis 50:20).

Because God is good, this statement is always true. When we look back with eternal perspective we will be able to see that in all of our difficult times "God intended it for good" could be written over every detail He allowed.

Unanswered prayer may be God's way of leading us into a more fruitful life. A godly minister had an only child who was at the point of death. When the doctor informed these parents there was no hope their son would live, their hearts rebelled against God and in their anguish cried out that God was unkind.

Then the Holy Spirit reminded them that God is love and gave them grace to accept whatever God allowed. The father said, "We must not let God take our child. We must give him." So kneeling at the bedside, they humbly gave back to God the child He had loaned them for a short time.

The fragrance of Christ came into their lives in a fresh way. Every person in their congregation sensed a wonderful spirit in this fully surrendered couple. We, like Moses, may not know our faces (and our lives) are shining when we accept God's kindness in whatever form He allows, but others will know and be blessed.

Good when he gives, supremely good.
No less when he denies.
Afflictions from his sovereign hand
Are blessings in disguise.
—Anonymous

One of the tenderest names God used for Himself was *El Shaddai*. The Almightiness of God is expressed in *El*, a short form of *Elohim*, which means "the Mighty One." *Shaddai* suggests perfect supply and perfect comfort. It could be rendered "God All-

43

Sufficient." It suggests exuberance, sufficiency, bountifulness, and perfect satisfaction, all combined with irresistible power!

Amazingly, *El Shaddai* is most frequently used in the book of Job. In difficult times it may seem that God is far from being the One who pours forth blessings. But our faith rests upon the assurance that in the end we'll say with joy, "He has done everything well" (Mark 7:37). In every situation He intends to pour out good on those who love Him.

Pain often allows us to see God's goodness more clearly than do prosperity and good health. Nine-year-old Darrell had been burned so terribly that all of his body except his lips and one blistered cheek were wrapped in sterile gauze. When his seared flesh was touched his screams could be heard far down the hospital corridor. One day another patient called out, "How can God do this to an innocent child?"

"Don't say anything against God!" Darrell's voice rang out. "When it hurts, God cries with me." "In all their suffering he also suffered," declared Isaiah (63:9 NLT).

Many times we cannot see God's goodness except through faith, but because we trust Him we know that He allows nothing except what He can use to bring good to us. As His children we can say with confidence, "Surely goodness...shall follow me all the days of my life" (Psalm 23:6).

Dear Gracious Father,

In the midst of my pain and difficulties, by faith I proclaim Your goodness. I may not see it or understand how You're working, but today I choose to

believe that in all things You work for
my good. In Jesus' name, Amen.

Discussion Questions

1. Has anyone ever answered your question before you completely stated it? Tell of an incident when you realized God's answer was on the way before you called upon Him.

2. Although you may have experienced disappointment with God because His answers weren't what you expected or wanted, how did you see God's goodness in it?

3. Perhaps you're exercising faith in waiting to see God's goodness. What Scripture will you hold and cling to for strength and comfort?

The Rewards of Passionate Prayer

"I will rejoice in doing them good" (Jeremiah 32:41).

When Acsah married Othniel, she urged him to ask her father [Caleb] for an additional field. As she got down off her donkey, Caleb asked her, "What is it? What can I do for you?"

She said, "Give me a further blessing. You have been kind enough to give me land in the Negev; please give me springs as well." So Caleb gave her the upper and lower springs (Joshua 15:18-19 NLT, repeated in Judges 1).

When I noticed this story of Acsah going to her father and asking for the upper springs was told twice in the Bible, I began to search for its significance. What practical lesson does God have for us?

Caleb had given his daughter Acsah and her husband the land called Negev. Negev means to be parched, and to her credit, Acsah was not content with dry land! Even if her husband was unwilling to follow through on her desire for springs of water she would do her best to secure for her family more than parched land. Her passion caused her to intercede for her family.

When Acsah got down from the donkey, in Hebrew culture, she was humbling herself before her father. She also showed humility by asking for the favor as a "blessing." Yet, she did this with confidence.

If we have the passion of Acsah we will not be content if our families are in a dry spiritual land. We will show our passion through humble but confident intercession.

In October 1999, we had the privilege of hosting my cousin Wesley Duewel in our home for a few days. One morning I asked if he would share the teaching he gives in his prayer seminars. One of his comments has stayed with me. He said we are living in the dispensation of intercession.

Much of the Church appears to be missing this opportunity for intercessory prayer. Dr. Duewel mentioned that while we have many wonderful choruses calling us to worship and praise, we have few that call us into burden bearing. Our worship is precious to Him, but He made us to be a kingdom of priests and one of the roles of a priest is to be an intercessor.

Jesus now lives to make intercession; intercession is His passion. I think we can assume that He wants to live a life of intercession through His body on earth as He does in Heaven. As He lives through us, intercession will be our passion.

Acsah's father said, "I am so thrilled you asked for the upper springs that I will give you the lower springs, too." Our Father also gives the lower springs to those who plead with Him for the upper springs. When we ask God for spiritual blessings, we find that He increases our natural joy as well. As my mother used to say, "It makes this life richer to live for the next!"

Acsah's story also reveals the reward God gives to parents who have passion. Her father Caleb was seeing the fulfillment of the promise Moses had made years earlier. "The land on which your feet have walked will be your inheritance and that of your children forever, because you have followed the Lord my God wholeheartedly" (Joshua 14:9).

Caleb followed the Lord wholeheartedly (with passion!) and Moses promised that his passionate obedience would reappear in his children. Not only would Caleb inherit Canaan; his children would, too! Caleb must have recalled Moses' promise and rejoiced to see his daughter's aspirations. God's greatest reward for parents' wholehearted obedience is to give that same passion to their children.

A few months ago I met a lovely Christian named Ruth. She told me, "People say to my parents, 'It's so wonderful that all of your three children love the Lord. How did you do it?'

"My parents reply, 'Oh, we prayed and trusted the Lord,' but other parents pray. The reason I am a Christian is that my parents lived the Word. Not only did they teach the Word, but it was who they were all the time. They are the best Christians I know."

Jeremiah would have described Ruth's parents as having "singleness of heart and action." He declared that it would be "for their own good and the good of their children after them" (Jeremiah 32:39). Her parents' sincere desire to please the Lord was rewarded with the fulfillment of Caleb's promise: "The land on which your feet have walked will be your inheritance and that of your children forever, because you have followed the Lord my God wholeheartedly" (Joshua 14:9).

Passion is shown not only through intercession but also through wholehearted obedience. "I ask no other sunshine than the sunshine of His face," wrote Elizabeth Clephane in *Beneath the Cross of Jesus.* That is passion.

> *Dear Merciful God,*
>
> *Thank You that You give the spirit of intercession. Fill me with the passion Acsah and Caleb had so I cannot be content with "barren land." I want all You have for me, so I come to you in humility and with passionate longing for you to do great and mighty things that will bring You glory. In Jesus' name, Amen.*

Discussion Questions

1. When have you asked God for something and He gave you much more?

2. What are you passionate about? Are you interceding for it?

3. What might keep you from doing so? What Scripture will help you to move forward?

49

Well Diggers & Wall Builders

"...constantly I remember you in my prayers at all times" (Romans 1:9b-10).

"His sermon was a masterpiece." "What skillful delivery from a teenager."

Peter's sermon had been impressive. We admired this young man of our congregation who was showing such promise.

Occasionally I'd wonder, "Who is praying for Peter? He appears to be maturing spiritually, yet he doesn't come from a Christian home and have praying parents. Whose prayers are supporting him?"

Then Peter began missing church. At first he blamed his 80-hour-week work schedule and illness, but soon no excuses were made. Some of us in our congregation sadly shook our heads and bemoaned our loss, but did anyone go to God as his intercessor? Did anyone pray for him? When I heard that Peter now says he is an atheist and has lost interest in

Christianity, my heart cries, "Why didn't I intercede for him during his crucial, decision-making days?"

In his book *Life Together*, Deitrich Bonhoeffer wrote, "A Christian fellowship lives and exists by the intercession of its members for one another, or it collapses." If we don't take seriously our responsibility to intercede for each other, we are likely to see cracks in our fellowship, corners breaking off that are difficult to restore.

The apostle Paul understood that prayer for each other is essential. Not only did he ask prayer for himself but also he wrote to the Christians he had nurtured, "We constantly pray for you." (2 Thessalonians 1:11a).

In Deuteronomy 6:11, God told the nomadic Israelites they would come to wells they had not dug. What a refreshment it must have been for the weary travelers to come to supplies of water that their own efforts had not created.

There are days when we are spiritually thirsty, but too busy or too faint to provide our own source of refreshment. When someone else prays for us, however, a well of living water is established. We can drink and gather strength.

My husband and I were married after his first year of medical school, and the next three years could have been dry and difficult. He studied night and day, was on call every third night for many months, and was rarely able to attend church.

Despite these desert conditions, we did not suffer drought. Exam times meant extra prayer times. Often on Friday nights, our unhurried Bible reading and prayer would last nearly the entire evening. We then began a practice we still continue, of drawing spiritual strength together by reading the Bible or another Christian book.

We discovered we were drinking from wells we had not dug. During those busy years, a dear, praying woman in our church would occasionally come to my husband and quietly say, "I'm praying for you every day." Here was the secret of our strength. She and others were digging wells for us. Those were days when we probably would have neglected to dig our own if others had not interceded for us.

When our youngest child entered first grade, I began a new era in my life. With my children in school, I found my prayer list lengthening because I had more time to bear others' burdens. As I allow God to increase my sensitivity to others, I am noticing many who are too faint to dig wells for themselves.

I see Mitch withdrawing from church, and his name is added to my prayer list. Betty has her hands full teaching 20 fifth graders, so I make a note to pray for her. Carla has a difficult time enjoying her three preschoolers, so she, too, will be remembered. New Christians are entitled to prayer support. The list grows and grows.

On one occasion, while praying for a missionary nurse in New Guinea, I felt impressed to ask God to enable her to lead someone to Christ that day in the clinic. Mail comes slowly from New Guinea, so it was two weeks before I received a blue aerogramme from the missionary nurse written the day I had prayed. That morning two men had come to Christ in the clinic. Intercession had helped dig a well from which others received eternal refreshing.

We need not only wells of refreshment and strength but also we need walls of protection. Prayers that build walls of protection include, "Lead us not into temptation," and the prayer Jesus prayed in John 17:15, "I pray not that you take them out of the world, but that you protect them from the evil one."

As a teen-ager, I experienced the protection of my mother's prayers when I dated a fellow who failed to meet her approval. Though she did not chide me, she did have one gentle talk with me. I knew my mother had taken this matter to her prayer closet when several days after our talk, I was no longer attracted to this young man.

Walls of protection may not always be welcomed. For example, during Lois' teen years, she dreaded for her mother to learn of her rebellious ways. She knew that her mother's prayers were effective. It was years before she recognized the value of those prayers.

We pray earnestly for friends to have that initial encounter with Christ, but do we pray as sincerely for them after they have come to Him? Judy had not been a Christian long when she was dealt a blow that would have discouraged even a more mature Christian. "I feel like giving up," she said.

That night my husband and I prayed for her, asking God to keep her from defeat. She later told me what happened to her that same evening.

She had felt like skipping devotions but found herself unable to do so. To her surprise, it was easy for her to pray. She arose from her knees encouraged.

During the next few days, as we continued to pray for Judy, God used a sermon at church, a phone conversation, and an invitation to assist in a church program to help her regain her joy in the Lord.

Paradoxically, digging wells and building walls for others do not lessen our own strength. On the contrary, we find ourselves growing in faith. It is as though all of the wells and walls we form become wellsprings and protection for our own spirits.

Paul's intercessory prayers for strength and refreshment in the first chapters of Ephesians, Colossians, and Philippians are prototypes to be used again and again by substituting names of those on our prayer lists. As we familiarize ourselves with the burdens on the apostle's heart, we'll learn to pray more effectively than "Bless Betty" and "Help Joe."

One of the keys to Paul's prayers was that he could testify, "I long for all of you with the affection of Christ Jesus" (Philippians 1:8). This loving concern and yearning will motivate us to pray in sincerity and faith.

In Israel's first battle, Moses sent Joshua to lead the army. Then he took Aaron and Hur and went up to the top of the hill to pray. Through the day, one fact became apparent. The armed soldiers did not determine the winning side. The prayer warriors determined it.

The great need of any group of believers is to have intercessors digging wells and building walls. We each can follow Jesus' example when He said to Simon Peter, "Satan has asked to sift you as wheat. But I have prayed for you, Simon, that your faith may not fail" (Luke 22:31-32).

Dear Heavenly Savior,

Please give me Your sensitivity to pray for those in need. Stir me to remember that another's spiritual well-being may depend upon my prayers. Empower me to be faithful in well digging and wall

building for Your glory. In Jesus' name,
Amen.

Discussion Questions

1. In 2 Corinthians 1:8-11 Paul tells of the hardships he suffered. How did intercessory prayer make a difference?

2. How is it that "digging wells and building walls" for others benefit our own spiritual lives?

3. Is God calling you to intercede for someone(s) at this particular time? Stop now and offer up prayers of faith. Consider praying Colossians 1:9-14.

Whose Battle Is It?

"The eternal God is your refuge, and underneath are the everlasting arms. He will drive out your enemy before you, saying, 'Destroy him!'" (Deuteronomy 33:27).

Joshua had been surveying the insurmountable wall of Jericho. Taking this city appeared totally impossible. Who of us has not faced one of those walls?

Then Joshua looked up. If he had studied only the problem, he would have gone home discouraged. God has a message of hope for all who look to Him.

In Joshua's upward look, he caught a vision of the Commander of God's armies with His sword drawn prepared to fight. We now know He was seeing Christ, but perhaps not realizing that supernatural help was before him, Joshua asked, "Are you for us or for our enemies?"

Joshua's question reveals a human way of thinking. "It's me against them. I have a battle to fight."

The Man answered, "Neither," or simply, "No," in the Hebrew.

Why wouldn't He be on Joshua's side? Wasn't Joshua the leader of God's people?

The message to Joshua was this: "I am Christ and I am always on God's side. This is His battle and I will fight for Him. He is interested in the outcome and is prepared to fight. You simply move at the command of the Lord and He will fight through you."

As my friend Brigitta commented, "Christ does not come merely to help us and certainly not to harm us; He comes to take full control! We must learn that the first step toward victory is to confess that we are second in command."

The question, then, was really to Joshua, "Whose side are you on?" God comes to accomplish His sovereign purposes, not our agendas.

Our fears melt away when we see that the armies of Heaven are ready and waiting to fight our battles for—or rather through—us.

"I used to ask God to help me," Hudson Taylor said. "Then I asked God if I might help Him. I ended up by asking Him to do His work through me." This is what Joshua was learning. The Commander was not there to help Joshua fight this battle; He was there to do the fighting through Joshua. There is a world of difference between asking God to help us do our work and allowing Him to do His work through us.

What must happen first? Joshua humbly begged, "What message does my Lord have for his servant?" Surely the Lord was about to give some important strategic details. But, no. First, Joshua must worship.

"Take off your sandals, for the place where you are standing is holy." Taking off his sandals not only expressed respect for the place, but also spoke of the reverence that our inner being owes to the holy God. Before we can allow God to use us to fight His battles, we must stand in His presence. We recognize that we are in His presence—right where we are! Anywhere we acknowledge His nearness is holy ground.

"This is a spiritual battle, Joshua, and you are not ready for it until you stand in the presence of a holy God."

Samuel Logan Brengle, an early Salvation Army minister who was mightily used of the Lord, understood this need well. When asked, "If you had but ten minutes to prepare for a meeting, how would you spend it?" Brengle replied, "In prayer." Brengle prepared to do God's work by first preparing his own heart. He wanted to spend time "with his sandals removed"—reverencing God in his heart.

After Joshua stood in the presence of the Lord, he was prepared to hear the Lord's assurance, "See, I have given Jericho into your hands" (Joshua 6:1). Even though God's instructions to march and blow trumpets did not appear to be a sure way to victory, Joshua was ready to follow directions and even boldly announce these seemingly preposterous plans to the Israelites. Amazingly, the people agreed to obey. They saw a leader who was fully assured God was leading. Of course they'd follow! When God is leading He puts it in people's hearts to do what He wants done.

Joshua received this word: Prepare yourself to allow Him to fight this battle through you. Acknowledge that where you are this moment is holy because God is with you. There is no better preparation for victory through Christ.

Dear Lord,

Thank You for Your gracious promise to do Your work through me. When I see a problem, may my first response always be to worship You and to trust You to fulfill Your purposes through me. In Jesus' name, Amen.

Discussion Questions

1. What "insurmountable mountain" are you facing today? Rather than taking control, what does God ask you to do so He can give you victory?

2. How will your approach to God change when you understand the difference between having God's assistance and allowing Him to do His work through you?

3. Worship was God's perquisite for Joshua before he could go out to fight. Why is it also necessary for us, so that God will receive our victory?

Never Too Old to Pray

"They shall still bring forth fruit in old age" (Psalm 92:14).

My Aunt Pearlie looked out her back window. Her green beans were up, and she knew the rabbits would appear any day. For years she had protected her beans by building a fence around them, but now in her seventy-second year, she found fence-building too much of an effort.

"Dear Lord, I'm tired," she prayed. "Would You protect my beans?" With a promise to give Him the glory if He answered her prayer, she left the beans to His care.

More days passed and one day Aunt Pearlie happened to notice that the rabbits were trespassing in her garden. But not once did they bother her beans! One day a neighbor commented on all the rabbits in her garden. "But they never go near your beans," he reported with amazement. The whole season Aunt Pearlie's beans were undisturbed.

Could it be that in the inevitable slowing down process of aging, God invites women to a greater life of faith and prayer? Anna, the first older woman mentioned in the New Testament, provides us a role model. "And she was a widow of about fourscore and four years, which departed not from the temple, but served God with fastings and prayers night and day" (Luke 2:73). What a fruitful life she must have had!

I'm reminded of another Anna, a ninety-six-year-old lady in a nursing home. For years Anna Bebermeyer pleaded with God to close a certain bar in her hometown of Warrenton, Missouri. The devastation it was doing to the people grieved her, so she begged God to remove this evil influence. About a month later, the restaurant unexpectedly announced it was closing its bar. What a miracle, but God wasn't finished!

Anna's pastor's wife had put a notice in the newspaper inviting anyone who wanted to learn more about the Bible to come to a Bible class. Soon her living room was too crowded, so she went to the local restaurant and asked if they could meet there.

They agreed and put the group in the very room where liquor had been sold only days before. God, who delights in giving exceedingly abundantly beyond what we ask or think, had given to her good measure, pressed down, and running over.

"I'm so happy, I want to clap my hands," this dear old lady said recently when her daughter visited her in the nursing home. But she can't clap her hands because of a stroke. About all she can do is lie in bed and pray. In fact, much of her time is spent in prayer.

Dear Lord,

Thank you for the older women who are living examples of faith and fruit-bearing. No matter what my age, I desire to keep praying, producing fruit that brings You glory. In Jesus' name, Amen.

Discussion Questions

1. Share how an "older" person's prayers have impacted your life, your community, or perhaps the world.

2. Write or call this person to encourage and thank her for prayers that have made an eternal difference.

3. What do you want to most characterize your life when you are older? Why?

The Key to Revival

"See I am doing a new thing! Now it springs up; do you not perceive it?" (Isaiah 43:19).

Could it be that we are beginning to see the fulfillment of God's promise in Zechariah 12 to pour out a spirit of grace and supplication? Not only are many new prayer groups springing up but also an increasingly large number report they are returning to the discipline of fasting.

In his book, *The Coming Revival*, Dr. Bill Bright tells of seeking guidance after sensing the Lord had called him to a 40-day fast. When he couldn't find information on how to conduct such an extended fast, he sought the Lord's wisdom. "Lord, I know You've called me to fast for forty days, but I can't find the help I need. I don't want to do anything foolish," he prayed. "Please help me!"

While he was seeking God's guidance, something extraordinary happened. He distinctly sensed a sobbing in his spirit; he knew the Lord was weeping. He was startled at first. And although he didn't know why He was weeping, Dr. Bright began to sob, too.

Then he sensed the Spirit saying, "My people have forgotten one of the most important disciplines of the Christian life, the major key to revival." He knew the Lord meant prayer with fasting.

The early church knew the value of fasting. Twice fasting is mentioned in Acts 13:2-3: "While they were worshipping the Lord and fasting, the Holy Spirit said, 'Set apart for me Barnabas and Saul for the work to which I have called them.' So after they had fasted and prayed, they placed their hands on them and sent them off."

This last verse says "they" sent them off. The next verse very significantly adds that the two were "sent on their way by the Holy Spirit." The Holy Spirit and the people were moving as one when fasting was combined with prayer.

More and more churches are encouraging fasting. I recently spoke with a lady who has been selected to be "prayer elder" in her church. One of her prayer goals is to have someone in their congregation fasting each day of the month for their church. She said she lacks only twelve people to have the entire month covered.

Another lady reported at St. Louis Prayer and Fasting that the Lord called her to fast one day a week for her church. On Wednesdays she only drinks water, and, amazingly, by the end of her workday, she feels better than on the days she eats. The Lord has given her a picture in her mind of her church with flames coming out of the top of it. She believes God wants to break out in revival in her church. Her hunger to know God's glory in their midst motivates her to fast.

God is giving desires to fast. A dear friend told me that she would be fasting for a week, and just before she began the fast, she wrote, "I know I'll have a wonderful time this week with the Lord. You know what? I didn't have any appetite for rich food, especially meat, for this whole week. It seems the Lord has taken it away to prepare me. He must have ordained my days."

Indeed He had! After her seven-day fast, she wrote, "I had no temptation for food at all during those days, no taste for it even though I prepared food for my son every day. My strength was unusual until the seventh day when I started feeling weak."

During the first day of her fasting, she watched Julio Ruibal's video on fasting and learned that he advised not to eat rich food for a week before fasting. The Spirit led her to do this before she watched the video!

Usually when I read in Zechariah 12 of God's promise to pour out a spirit of grace and supplication, I think only of the spirit of supplication. Recently, I wondered why He promised to pour out a spirit of grace. Grace is the desire and power to do God's will. How we need grace to pray and fast! We can call others to prayer and fasting and long to do it regularly ourselves, but unless God gives a spirit of grace and supplication (a desire to pray), little will be done.

In his excellent book *God's Chosen Fast*, Arthur Wallis says that our fasting must be God-initiated and God-ordained if it is to be effective. "On our part there must be the recognition of the rightness and need of fasting, the willingness for the self-discipline involved, and the exercise of heart before God; but in the final analysis the initiative is His. When we fast, how long we fast, the nature of the fast, and the spiritual objectives we have before us are all God's choice, to which the obedient disciple gladly responds."

"[Not in your own strength] for it is God Who is all the while effectually at work in you—energizing and creating in you the power and desire—both to will and to work for His good pleasure and satisfaction and delight" (Philippians 2:13 Amplified). Because it is God who gives us the desires we have, we should seek to respond to the desires He gives.

I recently longed so intensely for the Spirit's help that I began a fast. It ended after two days, but on the following day, I was amazed at the wonderful sense of intimacy I felt with the Holy Spirit. Then I remembered reading that one of the benefits of fasting is the increased communion with God that occurs either during or after a fast.

Why is God calling for more fasting, more prayer? Again and again, I return to Isaiah 43:19: "See I am doing a new thing! Now it springs up; do you not perceive it?" The Spirit is anticipating the fulfillment of God's promise to pour out His Spirit on all flesh. Do you not perceive it? Holy desires for prayer and fasting are springing up everywhere.

Dear Heavenly Father,

Please pour out Your spirit of grace upon me in order that I might fast according to Your will. I long to see Your kingdom come on earth as it is in heaven. I trust You will bring revival. In Jesus' name, Amen.

Discussion Questions

1. What do you think of the idea of fasting and praying for revival?

2. Why is it so necessary to ask for and receive a spirit of grace before fasting? Have you experienced fasting without it?

3. What personal benefits have you experienced by fasting?

An Instrument for Revival

"Blessed be the Lord, my Rock, who trains my hands for war, my fingers for battle" (Psalm 144:1).

In his excellent book *The Mind of Christ*, Dr. Dennis Kinlaw uses the Hebrew to define an intercessor as "a person who causes two other persons to meet." The picture is of a loving Almighty God on one side and a needy person on the other. God is looking for someone who can bring them together. I like to think that Christ is waiting at the entrance of each heart. He longs to speak, encourage, love, woo, and give wisdom, but He awaits our prayers, which give Him access to enter. Our intercession opens the way for the Holy Spirit to have access to another's heart.

Nancy responded to God's call to be an intercessor, and as He does for all of those responsive to such a call, He entrusted her with assignments. The following are just two of those assignments.

"After the Fasting & Prayer in Dallas, the Lord spoke to me on the flight home. He told me to do a prayer walk around the city where I live. Friends from my church join me, one at a time. Every week we go for about one to two hours. Our purpose is to saturate the neighborhood with prayer.

"Sometimes as we walk we see people in their front yards or working in their garages. We greet them and tell them we are walking around to pray for them and their households. Then, as the conversation continues and we recognize a specific need, we offer to pray with them. Usually they agree, though sometimes hesitantly. Most of the time their faces are changed after the prayer. Sometimes tears run down their cheeks. We also share the gospel when the Spirit leads us. If someone shows interest, we phone or visit them later.

"We begin praying for people we see in the distance and when we get closer we often find them ready for us to pray for them. For instance, we saw a young lady walking her dog. When we reached her, we learned her father had lost his job. Tears filled her eyes while we held her hand and prayed.

"One day we saw a group of five teenagers standing around a truck, looking somewhat arrogant. When we approached, we asked about such things as their schooling and then offered to pray for them. They began to giggle a little, but after prayer, we saw that they looked different. They appeared more thoughtful and respectful.

"Even kids 11 and 12 years of age are willing to let us pray with them. We often meet backsliders, and as we pray for them they look sober. Sometimes they express a desire to get back to church.

"I believe with all my heart that we walk where Jesus would walk and that Jesus has touched people through us. We do not need to see results because we believe the Spirit will continue His work in their lives."

After Nancy and her husband took their son to be admitted as a freshman in a Bible college, she said, "As soon as I stepped on to the campus, the voice of God came to me saying that this is another land He wants me to saturate with prayer. The next day He made it clear that He wanted me to spend a day every week on campus to pray for the faculty, staff, and students. I did not know anyone besides my son in the school at that time.

"The school gave me a small room called the Upper Room where I spend time with God on Fridays from 9:30 a.m. to 3 p.m. with a list of names of the students and faculty, and sometimes I am supplied with specific prayer requests.

"My door is open for whoever wants to come. Recently, two or three teachers came to pray with me for 15 to 30 minutes. Sometimes the campus pastor comes, and even some students have come.

"One teacher has come every time to pray for specific needs of her students. Recently she told me that one of them accepted the Lord. Another student had emotional problems and had been difficult to deal with. Yesterday I learned that he had changed. He suddenly became tender, humble, and open. He is not a Christian, but he has expressed that he needs God and asked us to pray for him. I believe he will know Jesus as his personal Savior soon.

"God may revive the campus through this little room. I humbly pray that I will continually be an instrument in His hand for revival just through the ministry of prayer."

Nancy anticipates God's answers. When God places a desire within our hearts, we can pray with joyful anticipation. He is eager to answer the requests He inspires us to ask.

The key to intercession is desire, a desire for more of God in our situation. But what should we do if we don't sense a strong desire to pray?

We do what we would do if we had desire. If we had a deep hunger for God to answer a prayer, we might pray regularly each day specifically for that person or need. We might forego some sleep or food. We would find a way to show God we are seeking Him with all our hearts.

The Holy Spirit will not force His assignments on us. He looks for the one, though, who through her prayers will bring together a compassionate God and the needs of others. He will trust that one with the desires of His heart.

> *Dear Gracious Father,*
>
> *I desire to pray for what's on Your heart and with Your passion.*
> *Strengthen my will to faithfully pray for the assignments You give. As I trust the Holy Spirit to help me, I anticipate Your answers. In Jesus' name, Amen.*

Discussion Questions

1. Intercessions are prayers for the needs of others, although sometimes we don't know how to pray. What encouragement does Romans 8:26-27 give you?

2. How have your intercessory prayers changed a life? A difficult situation?

3. If you lack desire to pray intercessory prayers, how should you proceed?

Recognize His Indwelling Presence

"We are the temple of the living God" (2 Corinthians 6:16).

My friend Beth shared that one morning after she awakened, she said, "Jesus, I'm in You and You're in me, and we're both in the Father through the power of the Holy Spirit."

That truth is too delightful to comprehend. A theologian once said that the greatest mystery, second only to the mystery of the Trinity, is the mystery of God's Spirit living within us—the indwelling Holy Spirit. Although we can never fully comprehend this awesome mystery, we can learn to enjoy it and delight in it.

The apostle Paul says it again and again, "I have been crucified with Christ and I no longer live, but Christ lives in me." He also stated, "God sent the Spirit of His Son into your hearts" (Galatians 4:6).

Because the Holy Spirit indwells, us we have the privilege of simply lifting our decisions and all our ways to Him throughout the day. He will direct us. "In all thy ways acknowledge him and he shall direct thy paths" (Proverbs 3:6 KJV). "In all thy ways!" I recall regretting a decision I had made, and the Holy Spirit gently reminded me that I had not acknowledged Him.

I understand what it means to acknowledge a friend when she enters a room. I turn to greet rather than ignore her. So when a situation comes in my path, no matter the size, I'm to acknowledge the Lord by saying, "Jesus, what about this?"

Someone asked A. B. Simpson, "What does it mean to abide in Jesus?"

Dr. Simpson replied, "It is to keep on saying minute by minute, 'For this I have Jesus!'" The unspoken implication is "For this situation I have Jesus and He is enough. He will provide the wisdom, peace, protection, guidance, and comfort—all I need." The more we acknowledge Him and delight in His abiding in us, the more we realize that, indeed, having Him is enough.

Even if we lack a sense of God's presence, the Spirit is in our hearts, and we should act accordingly. As we learn to acknowledge Him in all our ways, the consciousness of His presence will grow.

We often do not begin with feeling, but by faith we live as though He were within us. So if we desire to abide in Christ, we treat Him as if He were in us, and we in Him. He will respond to our trust and honor our confidence.

The Holy Spirit delights in guiding us. Surely most days He has more wisdom to give than we think to request. To the degree that we live with awareness, "The Lord is near" (Philippians 4:5) and recognize His presence and rest in Him, we abide in Him.

The abiding Holy Spirit wants to do much more than give us guidance and assurance. He wants to reveal Himself through us. I heard a mother tell that she had asked God to heal her daughter who had been seriously injured in an accident. "God, wouldn't it be wonderful if the doctor could see how wonderful You are by healing her?"

God replied, "Wouldn't it be wonderful if the doctor could see how wonderful I am by what I do in you?"

His indwelling is not only for our enjoyment but also for those close to us. God receives glory when we say, "For this I have Jesus and He provides all I need."

What if we sometimes simply forget to acknowledge God? We're like Joshua and the men of Israel who when asked to sign a treaty with the Gibeonites "sampled their provisions but did not inquire of the Lord" (Joshua 9:14). Those sneaky Gibeonites knew the Israelites were not to make a treaty with their next-door neighbors so they pretended to have come a long distance. They displayed their moldy bread and said it was hot out of the oven when they left home. They declared their worn-out sandals had been new when they started on their trip.

Why ask the Lord about this? The answer appeared obvious; surely these men did not live near them. Joshua and his men impulsively signed the treaty. Three days later they learned they had been tricked and soon they were called into war to protect the Gibeonites.

But God always leaves us with a word of hope. Even though their failure to "inquire of the Lord" resulted in a battle they would not have had to fight if they had acknowledged Him, God didn't say, "Well, you're on your own now. If you had only asked me, you wouldn't be in this fix."

When we fail to seek God's direction and we find ourselves in a mess of our own making, we are tempted to think God doesn't want to help us. That is not true and Joshua understood that. Soon the Israelites had to go to war to defend the Gibeonites, and Joshua had the boldness to ask for supernatural help.

This is the battle when "the sun stopped in the middle of the sky and delayed going down about a full day. There has never been a day like it before or since, a day when the Lord listened to a man" (Joshua 10:13-14). Even though Joshua had not listened to God, the Lord listened to Him.

What a loving Holy Spirit lives within us!

Dear Faithful Father,

What a marvelous gift I have received—the Holy Spirit living in me! Please help me to stay alive to Your presence. Forgive me for the times I have grieved You by ignoring You. Today, I desire to abide in You, moment by moment trusting You for guidance, wisdom, and understanding. In Jesus' name, Amen.

Discussion Questions

1. Is it really possible to abide in Jesus moment by moment? If we are to abide in Jesus, what mindset must we continually carry?

75

2. What if you don't *feel* His indwelling presence? How is it then possible to abide?

3. How might living with this awareness of His indwelling presence affect your life? Your family? Your community?

Be Still and Know

"One thing have I asked of the Lord, that will I seek after: that I may dwell in the house of the Lord all the days of my life, to gaze upon the beauty of the Lord and to inquire in his temple" (Psalm 27:4.)

I have enjoyed thinking about the Israelites' journey through the wilderness. "In all the travels of the Israelites, whenever the cloud lifted from above the tabernacle, they would set out, but if the cloud did not lift, they remained. So the cloud of the Lord was over the tabernacle by day and fire was in the cloud by night, in the sight of all the house of Israel during all their travels" (Exodus 40:38).

Imagine being an Israelite and always, every day, at each step of the journey knowing exactly which way to go. They never had to question, "I wonder where God wants me to go today." By day and night they had direction. It is true, though, that the Israelites had to be content to move at the timetable of the cloud. They might have felt, "I'm wasting my life just waiting for that cloud to move."

But they waited; they didn't rush ahead no matter how long the cloud stayed in one place. If the cloud did not lift, they did not set out. Their protection was in their obedience. If the Israelites had no longer been able to see the cloud, they would not have known the right way.

We read about their guidance and think, "Wouldn't that be wonderful?"

But more wonderful is having the reality of what that cloud by day and fire by night symbolized—the Holy Spirit. He is our constant Guide. With Him we have the possibility of enjoying constant communion. Then why do we feel lost at times? Why do we sometimes feel we need direction and don't have it?

Our problem is that we forget the cloud and pillar of fire. We act and think as though we don't have continual guidance and that there is no voice behind us saying, "This is the way; walk in it" (Isaiah 30:21).

One of the greatest privileges of Christians is the joy of sensing God's leadership, to clearly know when God is saying, "Hold it; don't move just yet," and to receive grace to respond to a Spirit-given hesitancy, an inner red light. Other times the Spirit gives clearness, an inner knowing, a green light that indicates, "This is the time, say those words, or make that purchase...."

If we don't sense any inner direction, it could be we haven't spent enough time in God's presence. The cloud in the Old Testament was a response to Moses' prayer in Exodus 33:15: "If your Presence does not go with us, do not send us up from here." God promised, "My Presence will go with you, and I will give you rest." Moses' refusal to go without

God's direction was the secret to their ability to know God's guidance.

Too often we don't wait for the cloud. We speak—but not at the impulse of the Spirit. We say what we think, not what the Spirit thinks. We grow weary and impatient, thinking we know the way, and we forge ahead, leaning on our own understanding. Because we are not being still enough to know God, our cloud is left behind.

In his excellent book *Hearing God*, Peter Lord tells of reading Hebrews 1:13: "Sit at my right hand, until I make your enemies a footstool for your feet." He first thought this verse applied only to Jesus, but after praying for a personal application, this is the answer God gave him.

"Peter, my Son Jesus is seated at my right hand, and you are raised up and seated with him (Ephesians 2:6). You have the privilege of sitting there with us (1 John 1:3). This is where your heart needs to be continually—seated in fellowship with me.

"Your trouble is that you are running around trying to take care of your troubles, your 'enemies' and I have to use my right hand to get you to sit down. If you would sit and fellowship with us you would set my right hand free to make your enemies your footstool. Come, my son, sit and fellowship with us, and we will take care of your enemies. Notice, you have not done too well at doing it yourself!"

What a joy to remember that our role is to fellowship with Him without worrying about our enemies such as fear or lack of wisdom.

Last month when I attended the monthly meeting of Kansas City's City-wide Prayer Movement, someone prayed something like this: "Thank You for this day of communion," and the Holy Spirit said to me,

"When you get up in the morning, don't think, 'I have this and this and this to do,' but think, 'Another day for communion with God!'"

Attend to the Lover Within You. These words were on my mind when I awakened one Sunday morning. With these words came a picture of the previous evening. I had been away for several days, and it had been so good to return home and focus on family. Our daughter and son-in-law had come over and as we sat around the table eating strawberries and ice cream, I "attended" to them. I was eager to absorb their words and to concentrate on what they shared about their days while I was away.

As I thought of our visit, I understood what the Spirit wanted me to do. Absorb His words, be attentive to Him, abide in Him, and listen to His words of love.

My friend Dorothy said that she had read someone's suggestion, "Let God love you." She realized how frequently she told God she loves Him, but how seldom she allowed Him to love her. There is strength in attending to the One who indwells us.

As we attend to the One within, we will discover the cloud by day and the fire by night!

Dear Heavenly Father,

What a privilege to be seated with you! When I forget this, I forfeit our sweet communion. Help me to gaze upon Your beauty more than anyone or anything else. Above all things, I want to give You first place in my life. I long to be still and hear You tenderly tell me, "I love you." In Jesus name, Amen.

Discussion Questions

1. Am I aware of God's presence? What does having an awareness of His continual presence look like in my life?

2. When God speaks, am I listening? How has He spoken to me lately?

3. What keeps my heart from being still in order to enjoy sweet communion with Jesus?

Victorious Prayer

"Here is my servant, whom I uphold...I will put my Spirit on him" (Isaiah 42:1).

"I'm in a prayer group at church, and I think 95 percent of our prayers go unanswered. The other 5 percent are prayers we pray for things, such as guidance, and we assume God answered. But maybe those things would have happened anyway. I have been reading promises about prayer: 'Ask whatever you wish, and it will be given you' and 'Ask and you will receive,' and I just don't see God answering like that. If only He had said, 'Most of your prayers will be answered,' I could accept that, but everything? I find these verses to be....'"

"Discouraging?" I asked when the young mother paused.

"Yes, well, at least challenging."

For the next 30 minutes we discussed how to pray the prayer of faith. God always keeps His promises to defend His own name. When someone asked a

Scottish lady, "But what if God fails you?" she responded with good theology: "He would lose more than I would." God's character and glory rest on His faithfulness because His kindness to us will be on display for all eternity (Ephesians 2:7). We can be sure there will be no hint of a flaw in that display. How, then, can we pray the prayer that always obtains the promise?

In 1 Chronicles 5:22, God's people won the war because the battle "was of God" (KJV). Whenever the Israelites sought the Lord regarding which battles to fight and then went at His command, they always had victory. On the other hand, if they went without His leading, they lost the battle.

Prayer is our battleground, and we, too, must expect God to help us know which battles are "of God." My friend Marjorie frequently speaks on prayer, and told me she once asked a group, "How would you pray for a 15-year-old put into prison unjustly?" After the discussion she told them the young man she referred to was Joseph. While we might have thought an instant release would have been the best answer, God's delay brought Him more glory and Joseph greater good.

Sometimes when we begin to pray, the Holy Spirit lets us know our request would not fulfill His desire. It is as though He says, "You mean well, but I have a higher desire." As we continue to pray, often exact words will form in our minds, words that we recognize the Spirit is pleased for us to pray. It may simply be a heartfelt, "My deepest desire is for You to be glorified in this situation."

If that is our desire in prayer, we do not care about the way God answers our request. As George Mueller stated, the way God chooses to answer is so unimportant to us that we would not turn over our hand to change the outcome. Our only concern is that the answer be His choice.

Because we "do not know what we ought to pray...the Spirit intercedes for the saints in accordance with God's will" (Romans 8:26, 27). We may be unaware that our prayers are not expressing our desire for God to receive glory. The Spirit has been given to help us know how to pray, so we should be careful not to ignore His help.

When the Spirit places His desires in our hearts then we can and should pray until we know He has heard. As Hannah Whital Smith said, it would be foolish to think that a person we are talking with can assure us she has heard our request but doubt that God can assure us He has heard. John implies this "knowing" is possible when He says, "This is the confidence we have in approaching God; that if we ask anything according to his will, he hears us. And if we know he hears us—whatever we ask—we know that we have whatever we asked of him."

To "know he hears" requires persevering in prayer. In fact, the word "ask" in that verse means to crave or to desire. When we see that we can do nothing of any value unless we do it through Christ, when we realize that all is lost unless God answers our prayer, when Jacob's words, "I will not let you go unless you bless me" (Genesis 32:26) become our heart's cry, then, and not until then, will God "see the travail of [our] soul and be satisfied" (Isaiah 53:11 KJV). These words in Isaiah were spoken prophetically of Jesus Christ, and we are now Christ's body on earth.

Then, knowing He has heard, we can say with confidence, "It is done." God calls things that are not as though they are. "I have given them into your hands," he told Joshua before the battle. The actual fighting had not taken place, but God saw all His conditions were met, so He knew He could lead them to victory.

An amazing phrase is repeated in 2 Samuel 8. "The Lord gave David victory everywhere he went" (vs. 6, 14). Earlier David had prayed, "Do as you promised, so that your name will be great forever." When the desire for God's name to be honored is the basis for our persevering prayers, God gives continual victory 100 percent of the time.

> *Dear Faithful God,*
>
> *Help me to enter into the battleground of prayer with confidence, trusting that You have heard. I trust the Holy Spirit to guide me into the specific prayers that express Your desires. Now as I submit my requests, I praise You for answering in whatever way gives You the greatest glory. In Jesus' name, Amen.*

Discussion Questions

1. God always keeps His promises to defend His name. According to Romans 8:31-32 why is this true?

2. What insights have you gained about praying prayers that always obtain the promise?

3. If you agree with George Mueller's comment that "the way God chooses to answer is so unimportant to us that we would not turn over our hand to change the outcome. Our only concern is that the answer be His choice," how might that change your prayers?

Will You Unite in Prayer?

"May they be brought to complete unity to let the world know that you sent me and have loved them even as you have loved me" (John 17:23).

Matthew Henry said, "When God intends great mercy for His people, He first of all sets them to praying."

God is indeed setting His people to praying. A few years ago a couple in South Africa felt God calling them to coordinate a prayer movement that has now become Global Day of Prayer. The mission of this movement is monumental: "To call Christians from all nations to unite in repentance and prayer, and to collaborate as God's instruments for the blessing and healing of the nations." Such an extraordinary goal requires the fire of the Holy Spirit given at Pentecost. Their theme proclaims: "Prayers Toward a Greater Pentecost."

The first global day of prayer was May 15, 2005. Estimates indicate believers gathered in approximately 10,000 events worldwide in 156 nations. Many countries reported amazing results.

One of those is Mali, a semi-arid region of West Africa. Drought and famine are fearful plagues in this country. Famine struck several countries in 2005 due to the meager rains and the locust invasion in 2004.

The churches in Mali decided to intensify praying by fasting for two weeks, from May 1-14, 2005, with their prayer and fasting culminating on May 15, the Global Day of Prayer. That day many churches in cities throughout Mali hosted prayer gatherings. Over 1000 believers, including some government officials, gathered in the Culture Palace of the government. Various ones came forward to pray for a specific issue facing the nation. Rain was the critical need.

By the time the meeting finished it was raining. One government official announced, "It has already begun!" Rain continued to pour down regularly. At the time of the report farmers were already beginning to harvest maize, and other crops looked promising. No locust invasion had been reported. They knew the Lord of lords had answered their prayers.

Another prayer movement that is sweeping through the world is the 24-7 prayer movement that began in London. Pete Grieg, the founding catalyst for this international call to prayer, said there is something unprecedented happening. Streams of prayer are arising day and night all over the earth. Pastor Gary Schmitz in Kansas City heard of this 24-7 prayer movement and bravely opened a prayer room hoping to get people signed up for one week of 24-7 praying. By about the fourth day there were so many stories of life transformation they began to realize that this is not simply a program. Consequently, their church prayed 24-7 for more than three months.

Pastor Schmitz resigned his church to work full-time with the City-wide Prayer movement in Kansas City to call more and more churches to 24-7 praying. Prayer rooms began springing up all over the city in practically every denomination.

Another group, Campus Transformation Network, has organized an amazing 24-7 prayer vigil for college campuses. Over 70 colleges are involved in the U.S. and recently 100 campuses in China joined as well. Jeremy Story, president of this group, describes their mission as saturating college campuses with God's glory and becoming a catalyst for transformation. By joining, students commit to coordinating a 24-hour prayer room to ensure every minute of the semester is covered in prayer for worldwide revival on college campuses.

J. Edwin Orr, speaking at the National Prayer Congress some years ago, said, "There has never been a spiritual awakening in any country or locality that did not begin in concerted united prayer."

God speaks of the synergistic power of united prayer when He says, "Five of you will chase a hundred, and a hundred of you will chase ten thousand" (Leviticus 26:8). Deuteronomy 32:30 speaks of one man chasing 1000 and two putting 10,000 to flight. Results are multiplied when two or more join together in prayer. God values unity so much that it's as if He says, "If you unite in prayer, I will abundantly reward you!"

Let's join together in praying for a spiritual hunger for holiness, believing His promise: "If two of you on earth agree about anything you ask for, it will be done for you by my Father in heaven. For where two or three come together in my name, there am I with them" (Matthew 18:19-20).

Dear Holy God,

May Your spirit fall fresh upon me this day. Use my prayers united with others for a greater Pentecost to saturate this world for Your glory! In Jesus' name, Amen.

Discussion Questions

1. Prayer is a perquisite for releasing God's abundant mercy. In what ways have you observed God's mercy poured out because of Your prayers?

2. In Matthew 18:19-20, Jesus instructs you to pray the prayer of agreement. Why?

3. When unity in prayer takes place, why do you think God responds so powerfully?

Pray Scripture

"For the word of God is living and active. Sharper than any double-edged sword, it penetrates even to dividing soul and spirit, joint and marrow, it judges the thoughts and attitudes of the heart" (Hebrews 4:12).

"Seek out the book of the Lord and read: no one of these [details of prophecy] shall fail" (Isaiah 34:16 Amplified). John Wesley interprets this verse to mean that if we pursue God's Word, "You will find that all things exactly come to pass as I have told you." God always fulfills His Word perfectly.

To learn what to pray, I pay close attention to Paul's prayers. Paul frequently began his letters by telling those to whom he was writing what he prayed. Certainly God answered those inspired prayers and will for us, also.

On the surface we might think his prayers are rather general and wouldn't apply to those for whom we pray. On the contrary, Paul requested exactly what produces spiritual maturity in all Christians. Who of us wouldn't want someone to pray that we'll be strengthened by His Spirit so Christ may dwell in our hearts through faith? (See Ephesians 3:16-19.) Frequently he requested that they grow in spiritual wisdom and understanding. Reflection upon Paul's requests enables us to see how shallow our requests often are.

Paul's prayers encourage me to offer requests I otherwise would not have considered. For instance, I noticed that he told the Corinthians he prayed they "will not do anything wrong....our prayer is for your perfection" (2 Corinthians 13:7, 9). These are prayers I now regularly pray.

Paul assures us in Philippians 4:19 that God will supply all our needs according to His glorious riches in Christ Jesus. It is appropriate that we turn such promises into confident petitions: "Meet all his needs according to Your glorious riches in Christ Jesus." Praying Scripture increases our confidence, and we discover that through "faith in him we may approach God with freedom and confidence" (Ephesians 3:12).

Wanting to pray Scripture increases our desire to memorize God's Word. The June 1996 issue of Taiwan Tapestry, a missionary newsletter from Drs. Ed and Connie Palm, challenged me. In it Dr. Connie Palm interviewed Dr. Louis Jan, one of their church leaders who spearheads a Bible memorization program. Some of the people in their church are memorizing chapters, even books of the Bible. Dr. Palm asked him why.

Dr. Jan replied, "Christians should memorize the Bible systematically so they can meditate on God's words anytime, anywhere. Joshua 1:7-8 says we are to have the law always in our mouths."

Those who are serious about making His Word available for prayer and meditation invest time. During the first week, Dr. Jan reads the chapter 50 times, then he studies it. The second week he memorizes it and finally recites it.

Author and friend, Mark R. Littleton writes, "I have found in my own life that Bible memory work carries with it a consuming hunger for more." Currently he is working on memorizing the entire New Testament.

Littleton travels 45 minutes each way to and from work, using much of that time to memorize God's Word. "Ask yourself," he suggests, "'what time during the day can I double up on or use to greater advantage?' A fast sandwich at lunch can give you time for a soul-filling meal of Scripture."

God's Word will never return to Him empty, but will accomplish what He desires and achieve the purpose for which He sent it (Isaiah 55:11). In verse 10, God gives an object lesson. He says His Word is like the rain and the snow that comes down from heaven and does not return to it without watering the earth. Imagine the rain beginning to fall and then returning to the skies before touching the ground. It is just that impossible for His Word to fail to accomplish what He desires.

Dear Lord,

Please teach me how to pray effectively by using Your Word. You are showing me that it's full of priceless treasures, ready and available to appropriate for blessing others. Thank You for never failing to fulfill Your Word. In Jesus' name, Amen.

Discussion Questions

1. Share some benefits you've experienced from memorizing Scripture.

2. What Scripture promises have you prayed that accomplished that which glorified God?

3. Why is it always "safe" to pray Scripture prayers according to Isaiah 55:11 and Isaiah 34:16?

Ask Boldly

"I will do whatever you ask in my name, so that the Son may bring glory to the Father. You may ask me for anything in my name, and I will do it" (John 14:13-14).

This past Easter I awakened early and opened my Bible eager to reread the account of Christ's resurrection. Before I reached the story of the empty tomb my Bible fell open to Daniel 7. As I read, I wondered, *Could this have been the scene in Heaven on that first Easter morning?*

"In my vision at night," wrote Daniel, "I looked, and there before me was one like a son of man, coming with the clouds of heaven. He approached the Ancient of Days and was led into his presence.

"He was given authority, glory and sovereign power; all peoples, nations and men of every language worshiped him. His dominion is an everlasting dominion that will not pass away, and his kingdom is one that will never be destroyed" (Daniel 7:13, 14).

Bible scholar Matthew Henry suggests that this appearance of Jesus occurs at the Ascension when the disciples saw Jesus disappear in a cloud (Acts 1:9), and certainly this may be true. Adam Clark, however, states that Jesus applied at least part of this verse to Himself before the Ascension when He said, "All authority in heaven and on earth has been given to me" (Matthew 28:18).

Even though we may be unsure of the exact timing of Jesus receiving all authority, glory, and sovereign power, we do know that at this moment He holds that power. Paul writes that Jesus is now seated at the Father's "right hand in the heavenly realms, far above all rule and authority, power and dominion, and every title that can be given, not only in the present age but also in the one to come. And God placed all things under his feet and appointed him to be head over everything for the church" (Ephesians 1:20-22).

We read on and learn an even more amazing truth. We, too, are seated with Jesus in this place of authority! "And God raised us up with Christ and seated us with him in the heavenly realms in Christ Jesus" (Ephesians 2:6). Paul prayed that the Ephesians would know they had access to this incomparably great power.

Occasionally we hear of those who discovered the authority available to all of us through faith. Missionary John Knight reports that while in Taiwan they moved across the lane, on an island near a man they later learned was the high priest of the Taoist temple.

Soon after they moved into this house they noticed strange things taking place, barely noticeable at first and quite inexplicable. His wife Cora became sick with a bright red stripe going up her arm, which, they learned was blood poisoning. Their daughter broke out in a terrible wet rash around her neck, and one day their son came running into the house screaming, with hands fully swollen. They felt a terrible oppression all around them.

Just as the Knights were about to go to the hospital in Taipei, they decided to fast and pray instead. On the third morning of their fast, they began to plead the blood of Christ to cover them and protect them from harm.

Soon after this they heard that the priest across the lane had boasted to someone that he was going to drive them off the island. They began to understand why these strange things were occurring. The priest had been using occult power to bring them harm. So, they began to plead the blood of Jesus Christ to cover this man and his house.

The effects were nearly instantaneous. Within two months they were in good health and still living on the island, but the priest and his family had unexpectedly moved away!

"They overcame him by the blood of the Lamb and by the word of their testimony" (Revelation 12:11). Pleading the blood of Christ is Scriptural and is one of the weapons of our warfare. The second weapon mentioned in this verse is the word of our testimony, testifying to what the Word declares to be true.

I visited with my niece, Ruth Ann Winters, whom God has used, along with her husband, to help save more than 70 souls through personal evangelism during the past year. She shared that her desire to win souls was granted after she began praying the Word with faith. A book by Ruth Shinness, *Prayer Strategy Resource Book*, encouraged her to paraphrase Scripture in a way that combines the Word with thanksgiving. For instance, Mark 1:17 KJV says, "Jesus said unto them, Come ye after me, and I will make you to become fishers of men." Ruth Ann would pray with faith, "Because I follow after You, Jesus, You have made me to become a fisher of men." "But you will receive power when the Holy Spirit comes upon you," in Acts 1:8 would be prayed, again with faith, "Thank You that I have received power, for the Holy Spirit has come upon me." After Ruth Ann began praying these Scriptures regularly, the Lord fulfilled His Word.

I happened to see a list of people filling one page in the back of Ruth Ann's Bible and I asked, "Are those people you have won to the Lord?" She smiled and nodded.

Is such praying being presumptuous? Only if we are praying outside of the Father's will. We are not to pray a request just to fulfill a selfish desire.

When the answer to all our prayers is simply for more of God and His will in our situation, then He invites us to come to Him with confidence (Hebrews 4:16) and ask anything (John 14:14; 16:23, 24).

Dear God,

I praise you today for Your precious blood, Your resurrection power, and Your powerful Word. Help me to ask boldly and with authority and with faith. I believe You will work in such a way that exceeds what I can think or imagine according to Your good pleasure and perfect will. In Jesus' name, Amen.

Discussion Questions

1. On what scriptural basis do you have the "right" to ask boldly?

2. How do you know if you are praying a selfish request or praying according to God's will?

3. On what condition will all your prayers be answered? Consider John 14:13.

How Do We Ask, Seek, and Knock?

"For every one who keeps on asking receives, and he who keeps on seeking finds, and to him who keeps on knocking it will be opened" (Matthew 7:7 Amplified). "Keep on asking and it will be given you." Bruce Wilkinson states in the Prayer of Jabez calendar that we are to think of God as a frustrated philanthropist. His generosity is continually thwarted because we fail to simply ask. God wants us to look to Him for everything and gives this amazing invitation, "Casting the whole of your care—all your anxieties, all your worries, all your concerns, once and for all—on Him; for He cares for you affectionately, and cares about you watchfully" (1 Peter 5:7 Amplified). Not a single one of our anxieties, worries, or concerns is too small to take to Him.

Anita is a new Christian I meet with for Bible study, and last week she told me what had happened just before I arrived. She had lost her keys two weeks earlier and had looked for them many times. Then at 10:30 she realized, "Aletha will be coming at any minute to get me; I must find my keys." She said, "I began praying, 'God help me find the keys,' and it came into my mind to look in a certain jacket. I had looked there many times, but this time I looked in a different pocket and they were there! I had not prayed about the keys before. God is so good! I had to thank Him!"

We have not because we ask not according to James 4:2. God is eager for us to ask and to keep on asking, either until we have the answer or until we know He has heard and are confident that the answer is on the way.

"Keep on seeking and you will find." I think of seeking as going a step beyond asking for our daily needs. It is in seeking God that He promises, "You will seek me and find me when you seek me with all your heart" (Jeremiah 29:13). We are seeking His will, His plan no matter what that may be. Seeking includes listening to the Spirit so we know exactly what to ask, surrendering to His will, and thanking Him for His perfect provision. How He decides to answer is fine with us—as long as we know His will is being done. Our motto is, "I'm satisfied if You are glorified."

When seeking God we are sensitive to what pleases the Holy Spirit. Sometimes we may ask for something to which God would say, "You mean well, but I have a larger answer than what you can now see. For a while it may look as though I have not heard your prayer. Some day, though, you will be able to look back and know that I gave you the best possible answer."

We reply, "Dear Lord, I trust You to give what is good even if it does not appear to be good at the moment. Your purposes are higher than mine." If we seek God with all our hearts, then one part of our heart will not want God while another part wants our own desire. We wholeheartedly want His highest plan. "Keep on knocking [reverently] and the door will be opened to you." Knocking signifies we want access into His presence where we discover the joy of communion with Him. When we knock, the door is opened, and what wonderful sweet fellowship we can have with Him! He is eager for our communion! When Jesus told the disciples, "I have eagerly desired to eat this Passover with you" (Luke 22:15), He used an emphatic word for eagerly. He was saying, "I have set my heart upon having communion with you." Jesus is still longing for our times of loving fellowship with Him.

In the preface to *The Knowledge of the Holy,* A. W. Tozer writes that we have lost our ability to withdraw inwardly to meet God in adoring silence. Yet those who reverently knock, longing to express their love to Him and to receive His love, find that the door will always be open.

After Jesus died, perhaps Mary Magdalene, from whom Jesus had cast seven demons, felt the loss more than the others. Peter could go back to fishing, but Mary didn't have a life before Jesus. Her heart must have been longing for His presence when she went to the garden that Sunday morning. Jesus arose from the dead, and because His full surrender of Himself had been first of all to His Father, He must go to Him first.

Yet, it seems almost as if Jesus broke protocol when He stopped by the Garden and spoke to Mary on His way to His Father. Jesus' heart could not resist Mary's deep desire for His presence.

Christ still responds to us when we draw near to Him in our spirits. I love Paul's phrase in Colossians 3:4, "Christ, who is our life..." The inner joy we can have because of a consciousness of His divine Presence is, indeed, life!

What beautiful invitations Jesus gives us: Ask, seek, and knock. When we do, we discover the door into His presence wide open, and we receive His blessings and find God's best for our lives.

> *Dear Lord,*
>
> *Today, I come into Your presence, asking, seeking, and knocking. I cast all my cares and concerns upon You, believing you will attend to every need I have. I believe You will give to me Your absolute best. Thank you for warmly welcoming me into Your presence. There is nothing I enjoy more than my intimate times alone with You. In Jesus' name, Amen.*

Discussion Questions

1. Sometimes we fail to ask because we think our request is too small or too insignificant, like a request for lost car keys. How does 1 Peter 5:7 address this obstacle?

2. The kind of seeking God is looking for requires an undivided heart. In your own words, describe an undivided heart.

3. Do you deeply desire your heavenly Father's presence? Take a moment to tell Him and then simply let

Him know how much you love Him. Experience His warm embrace.

Notes

Notes

Notes

Notes

Notes

Notes

Notes

For more books for individual and small groups,
visit www.cometothefire.org.